Little Pumpkin Pickers

The Cow Boss Series
By Karen Kasper

Halo Publishing International

Copyright© 2016 Karen Kasper
Photos by, Stephanie Lynn Photography
All rights reserved.

No part of this book may be reproduced in any manner without the written consent of the publisher except for brief excerpts in critical reviews or articles.

ISBN 13: 978-1-61244-510-6
Library of Congress Control Number: 2016917395

Printed in the United States of America

Published by Halo Publishing International
1100 NW Loop 410
Suite 700 - 176
San Antonio, Texas 78213
Toll Free 1-877-705-9647
www.halopublishing.com
www.holapublishing.com
e-mail: contact@halopublishing.com

As I anxiously made my way through the entangled vines of my pumpkin patch to see what surprises I would harvest this year, there it was, one Great Pink Pumpkin! I didn't specifically plant pink pumpkins, so how did this happen? WOW! How appropriate that this pumpkin presented itself in October, breast cancer awareness month.

As my 31-year-old niece, a mother of three, begins her treatment for stage IV breast cancer, this book idea presented itself. It was a symbol and sign to take this opportunity to write a personalized story book for my niece and her family.

I've decided to donate a percentage of these book proceeds to my niece's family for medical expenses and a percentage to breast cancer research. By purchasing this book, you're not only spreading the love of reading, you're supporting the Stronger Together Movement. Thanks for your support!

Welcome to our farm and pumpkin patch day,
Everyone get ready, let's be on our way!

Brynlee and Paige aren't wasting any time.
They're anxious to go and see what's under all those vines.

The girls were quick to pick some pumpkins and gourds, but Miss Brynlee couldn't quite decide which one she adored.

Grandma and Brynlee found a little pumpkin so cute, but Brynlee said "eww, it's all covered with dirt!"

Oooh what a great pumpkin so big and so round, but then Carter discovered he couldn't lift it off of the ground.

Cohen and Carter tackled one together, they laughed and said "this is definitely not as light as a feather! "

Little Harrison toddled around and around, and then he spotted a good place to sit down.

Milo admired this peanut looking pumpkin, but mommy decided it was too big for her little munchkin.

Then mommy and Milo found just the right one, with a little vine attached and not weighing a ton.

Reese was excited to show mommy her find, and they agreed that it was one of a kind.

Everyone load up and jump in the gator,
there is so much to see before you leave later.

Cohen made friends with two little kittens, appropriately he named them Tabby and Mittens.

He called over for Reese to cuddle them too, but clowning around was a trick that he knew.

Calves and cows is what this farm has,
so at lunch we will pour milk in everyone's glass.

There is one pig with black spots on his back, who gave a loud oink because he wanted a snack.

The giant hay bales were noticed by Cohen, Grandma approved them for jumping but warned "no bones broken!"

Little baby Milo also begged to get up,
he didn't want to be left out and neither did the pups.

Piper and the two boys sat high in the air, enjoying the action on that great big chair.

After much running, shouting and jumping about, they had to lie down, they were all tired out.

Carter, Harrison, Paige and Reesey,
Enjoyed the porch swing despite the squeaking.

The dinner bell rang to alert them for lunch, everyone had a big appetite and ate a whole bunch.

Time to go home and put the pumpkins in place,
After they are carved or painted a cute little face.

We thank you for coming and sharing the day,
drive safely and come visit again we say.